To

Thank you for inspiring us inspire me!

from.

David Rossiter

SHIPS
IN THE
NIGHT

DAVID ROSSITER

SOMEDAY BOOKS
LONDON

Published by
Someday books
London

First published in Great Britain 2012

ISBN 978-0-9573995-0-1

Words tumble over granite rocks,
They trickle to the sea,
Words sparkle in the sunlight
Reflecting you and me.

To Clair and Duncan
Who I love more than words.

Contents

Tomorrow Never Comes

Now,
It is over
In the blinking of an eye,
It has become a memory,
Fading, like a sigh.

This moment where we're living,
In an instant is the past,
Whose living recollections
Form reality so vast.

First love, first loss, first heartbreak,
The sunshine and the rain,
All live in this hereafter,
Again, again, again.

A Room with a View

Holiday vista through balcony bars
Cross seafarers' graveyard 'neath seafarers' stars,
Then ocean, horizon and infinite sky
Where some believe heaven awaits when they die.

Yet the journey is short to our ultimate fate
Which I see through these bars and the cemetery gate.
Behind balcony bars I am trapped on this side
With no heaven in view at the turn of the tide.

Cardinal Sin

A criminal institution
With rules of raffia;
The sickly smell of popery;
The holy mafia.

The plaster Virgin Mary weeps
To see the lowly beast,
Depraved, he wears the cassock,
Of a Roman Catholic priest.

The agony of Jesus Christ,
With blind enamel eyes,
Oblivious to child abuse;
Of innocence that dies.

A child's life is ruined,
The perpetrator free
To seek another victim;
Hidden by the See.

To pervert the cause of justice
The clergy must close ranks;
For the silence in the cloisters,
The pervert gives his thanks.

Our father is a paedophile,
Hallowed be his name,
Protected by the Vatican,
He is absolved of blame.

My Significant Other

A kaleidoscope of worries,
Like ubiquitous lost socks
That furtively exist within
A smoke filled paradox.

Fresh flowers in the dungeon,
Astro plastic lawn,
Enigma oxymorons
Will charge at break of dawn.

Ten Years Service

Cricket live from India
Showed flat screened on the wall
Above the boarded billiard table,
Ignored by one and all.

The company supplied the food,
Just six or seven plates,
Of bhajis, chips and sausage rolls,
To feed his working mates.

For Mr Singh was leaving,
He hadn't learnt his place,
And after his promotion
Had fallen out of grace.

They talked amongst themselves in groups,
He stood there on his own,
And even when they joked with him
He knew he was alone.

The boss then spoke of his ten years
Through which he'd worked and dealed,
The problems in his different roles;
The sausage rolls congealed.

And when it seemed judicious,
His mates began to leave,
They shook his hand and wished him well,
And flattered to deceive.

Postcard from Le Touquet

Sloping roofs, turrets on turrets,
The sunshine, pine trees and the rain,
Moules and chips and crashing waves,
Le Touquet calls, come back again.

The Yew

The churchyard – damp, ivy covered stones.
Mortality on show.
Lichen covered words will fade,
Yet seeds will shoot and grow.

Long wet grass surrounds the graves,
Beneath the yew it dies.
Dark green the branches bend and bow
To blacken out the skies.

Past generations saw this tree,
It stood to witness all.
Two thousand years or more it grew,
It watched us rise and fall.

No church stood here when it took root
In woods with boar and deer,
For Jesus Christ had not been born,
But Roman feet passed near.

The yew we see outlived them all,
Saw Jesus live and die.
Two hundred billion gone to rest,
Beneath this tree they lie.

Two hundred billion gone to hell,
Or entered heaven's gate?
The yew would know if *one* came back,
To indicate their fate.

Suppose

Suppose that Jesus was a man
Of leadership and charm,
Whose qualities made those in power
Afraid he'd do them harm.

Suppose the leaders of the church
Would rather see him dead,
So sought his crucifixion,
Subduing those he led.

Suppose it could take several days
To die upon the cross,
But Jesus died within six hours,
A premature loss?

Suppose that when his body lay
So comatosed and calm,
Within the safety of the tomb
His friends gave myrrh and balm.

Suppose that Jesus then revived
And friends then helped him leave,
Disciples saw his wounds and claimed
Immaculate reprieve.

Suppose that Jesus had to flee
But said he would return,
Then travelled east to old Kashmir,
Away from all concern.

Suppose through generations
His followers still wait,
To see his second coming,
In which they trust their fate.

Suppose that Jesus was a man
Of leadership and charm,
And not the prophet son of God
As hailed in book and psalm.

Suppose it's supposition
And all the faiths are factual,
Then we return back to a truth
Based on the supernatural.

Flotsam

I clambered inside my canoe
At the start of my career,
And paddled through a lifetime, swamped,
With crap and stress and fear.

Big John was more successful,
A rag-trade luminary,
Who felt he was secure with
All things pecuniary.

He's joined me now in car sales,
We're in a similar boat,
But he feels he has no paddle as,
Up shit creek we both float.

The Old Woman

Choosing to ignore her own mortality,
She sought to control her husband,
To his demise;

Maintaining her own existence
Upon the sinking foundations
Of his decline.

Unaware of her lack of kindness,
She feared losing him -
Whilst blaming him for going.

The Old Man

Strong enough to take the line of least resistance,
Yet it was a thin line,
Between keeping the peace
And total submission.

His faith kept him loyal,
Salvation was never in question,
He retained his quiet sense of humour,
- But the last laugh?

Old Computers

Metal shells of dust and must,
Of ageing oil and spider legs,
That plastic smell of yesterday,
Suspended future in decay.

That thirties semi without a gate,
A rusted useless toaster,
A private man in a hidden place
Of finger nails and yellow lace.

The World at Your Feet

A thinking ant you'd have to pardon
Who felt the cosmos was your garden
And microbes who begin to flirt,
Beneath your boot amongst the dirt

With concepts really not perverse,
Concluding dirt their universe.
But then it may be fair to moot
That we're beneath another boot.

In short that galaxies and star dust
Just make up a muddy crust,
Which sticks below some booted heel
Where it can dry and then congeal.

However, this boot and its world,
Will prove when things are then unfurled,
To be the muck beneath a shoe
Too vast to see by me and you.

But as we all have feet of clay,
To footwear, homage we must pay,
And thus pursue our hidden goal,
The preservation of our sole.

Conundrum Creation

All things bright and beautiful,
All creatures great and small,
With all our imperfections,
The Lord God made us all.

He made the stars, He made the earth,
Created Adam and Eve.
He made them good, He made them bad,
And able to conceive

Original sin which was passed down
Through all the generations.
He made the faults which caused the wars
And disunited nations.

But God is perfect, so He said
That sin was man's creation,
Then He sent down His only son
To stop the devastation.

Almighty God sent down His son
To die upon the cross,
Or was it God incarnate?
An even greater loss.

The crucifixion of the Lord
Atoned for all our sin,
But why could God not just forgive?
For He made everything.

My Mate's Cooker

My mate has been a looker
On e-bay for a cooker;
At 99p there's one he's seen,
The trouble is it's painted green.

Not what you'd call a hygiene fiend,
His old one he just never cleaned,
Congealed fat became so dire,
That one day the whole thing caught fire.

Since then it's lasted several years,
But now a new one he prefers,
As when he lights the front gas ring,
A fire breaks out from the front of the thing!

Inexorable Growth

As I sit here looking through
The nearly new glass patio doors,
I see the cracked walled flowerbed,
The summer heat within my head.

The garden may look rosy now,
But I see work ahead,
A tiredness within me knows,
I'm slowing down, while it still grows.

And what will happen when I die,
As weeds and ivy flourish?
I know the tide I cannot hold,
I watch them grow, as I grow old.

Yet even when I'm laid to rest,
Beyond all care and toil,
So roots will spread through flesh and bone,
To feed my ivy covered stone.

Knife

A sixteen year old
Lies in his blood,
I don't know his name,
Or who is to blame.

Knife removed,
Attackers gone,
He tells a passer-by,
He is afraid to die.

Cradled in a stranger's arms,
He calls out for his mum,
He's just a child who needs his home,
Instead he's dying, all alone.

Le Touquet
Tartlets and Tarantulas

Young girls of beauty on parade
Near fashion shops and palms,
Designer fabrics cover older,
Well married women's arms.

Expensive restaurants where they flash
Their smiles, as sharp as knives;
Expensive make up covers cracks,
Appearing in their lives.

Down pine tree shaded boulevards,
They walk small dogs on leads,
Suggesting that the lives they chose
Did not supply their needs.

The Spiral Staircase

The tower, tall and isolated,
Walls of cold damp stone,
In brooding contemplation,
Stands waiting, all alone.

In shadows dim, where spiders weave,
The spiral staircase climbs
And turns through dank and darkness
And turns a hundred times.

What horror lies behind the door
Atop the spiral stair?
Whose slippery steps will start to spin,
Then end, in locked despair.

A chink of light, an arrow slit,
Revealing desolate lands;
All locks are dead and rusted,
The keys in withered hands.

Buzzword

My wife says there's a wasp's nest
Up inside our roof,
I've been and checked- there isn't,
But she says she wants proof.

She says she'll get a man in
And pay him for his time,
Whilst she values my opinion,
My opinion is just mine.

She wants to get a proper man,
With wasps he'll have a knack,
I've decided that I'll kill her
And bury her out the back.

All Our Yesterdays

'Antiques Bought - House Clearances Offered'
Now closed 'Freehold for Sale'.
Glancing through the window,
A gloomy room, full of junk.

I never have bonded with antiques,
Just old tat covered in someone else's dust!
But here, spread before me lay
The contents of people's lives.

An ugly, ornate glass table lamp,
Decanters which once held the spirit
Of yesterday's better times
And over there, a rocking horse.

Sad and cold they lay,
Jumbled together, muddled and musty,
All left behind as poignant reminders
Of our own brief tenure.

Hell

Hell is the place where you go when you die,
Except if you're Catholic true,
So watch out if you're Muslim, a Buddhist or Sikh,
If you're Protestant, Hindu or Jew.

The sulphurous labyrinths are lying in wait,
Belching blood from their fiery bowels,
Eternity beckons to all but the few,
Through Hell's teeth and his putrescent jowls.

But I heard on the doorstep a definite fact,
That if you're a Jehovah's Witness,
You'll be saved in the end, but no one else will
Be considered of suitable fitness.

Muslims however all know very well
That they go to the Paradise Garden,
The rest are all infidels and have no chance
When they die of an Almighty pardon.

With that satanic organ playing below.
It's a bit like faith musical chairs,
When your music is finished if you pick the wrong one,
Then the furnace awaits you downstairs.

Now is it just possible all faiths are wrong?
And there's really no Heaven or Hell,
At the end of our lives just eternal peace,
Free of angst and religion as well.

Summertime in Cheam

Smile friendly sun, look down and beam
Upon the playing fields of Cheam,
Where holding hands on days like this,
The strolling lovers pause and kiss

And then gaze out across the green,
To where St. Dunstans church is seen.
That gothic spire, with ragstone hue,
Stands strong against a sky of blue.

From Nonsuch House the clock doth chime
To warn us of the passing time,
In which we fade from young to old,
As through the years our lives unfold.

In sunlit memories I recall
Our children back when they were small.
The playground, sandpit, and the swings,
And walks in Nonsuch Park like kings.

Since Tudor times the rising lark
Has sung its tribute to this park.
There is no fairer place it seems,
On earth - or even in our dreams.

Cards

Valentine, anniversary,
Birthday and Christmas,
We search for cards,
Then search for words.

Afraid to reveal too much
To those we know too little,
Afraid to express too little
To those we know too much.

We then exchange our attempts,
Showing love so sincere,
Or, maybe, somehow not so,
Then we display them to the world!

Eventually, putting them to one side,
For secret safe keeping, they stay,
Until death, or life, separate us.

Only then are they discovered,
Lying there, sadly,
In that drawer.

Ships in the Night

Cocooned in our own vessels
And blind to others' plight,
We sail through life's oblivion,
Like dark ships in the night.

Why do Angels have Wings?

Look to the horizon,
At the break of dawn,
It can be seen the earth is flat,
A line there has been drawn.

Above the clouds, is heaven,
The Godly firmament,
From where his holy messengers,
The Angels have been sent.

Gabriel came to Mary,
A virgin and a wife?
To say she'd bear the son of God,
And this may change her life!

When Gabriel saw Muhammad,
The above was then corrected,
Jesus was a prophet,
The 'son' bit was rejected.

A later revelation,
On tablets made of gold,
And given to a man named Smith,
Was definitive we're told.

And so it was that Christians
And Muslims spread their word
And later on the Mormons,
The truth that they had heard.

Above the clouds, in heaven,
With no atmosphere at all,
From grace, a host of Angels,
With wings, would surely fall.

Sharp Exposure

Sharp Edge invades my tired mind,
Flashing here through space and time;
Those gargoyled rocks in silhouette,
Look down from each sheer towering wall
Which meets at that serrated edge,
Exciting me, enticing me,
To make my pride become a fall.

I've looked down from Blencathra's peak
And peered up from its silent tarn;
I've braved Helvellyn's striding edge,
But this sharp malevolent place I fear,
Whose siren voice still beckons me,
Come to my edge, come close,
Come near.

The Oxfam Wedding Dress

The wedding dress, displayed
In the Oxfam shop window,
Begged so many questions.

Had he left her waiting at the altar?
Was there a tragic accident?
Or, had disenchantment quickly
Turned to indifference?

Maybe none of these.
Just needed more wardrobe space!
But why then, had she not kept
The small satin bag or that pretty tiara?

And who would purchase these symbols
Of purity, already twice given away?
A second timer on a budget, or,
Some hairy old transvestite from Leeds?

Perhaps, whatever went before,
The deepest sadness may lie,
Within the buyer.

Heaven

The Father Creator in Heaven abides
With His son and a ghost, who both sit at His side.
There are trillions of people all saved from their sin,
In His image created – like His next of kin.

Mary the Virgin is head of this throng,
With Joseph surrounded by Angels in song.
A heavenly aura lights halos and wings,
Whilst odours majestic are brought by three kings.

Archangel Gabriel takes charge of the Hosts
Of Cherubims, Seraphims, Dominions and most
Of the Powers and Virtues and thousands of Saints,
Principalities, Thrones all washed clean of their taints.

Beasts of the world all come here through space,
From hydra to whale, they all have their place.
The germ and the virus from centuries past,
All rise up to Heaven where all of them last,

Forever, together, in life evermore,
The good and the humble, the rich and the poor;
But logistics and crowding allow only souls,
As bodies need feeding and lavatory rolls.

Feather Jumpers

Pigeons seem to travel
From all points near and far,
Then casually they goose step
Beneath the wheels of my car.

Although they have a death wish,
Their course they quickly alter,
They fail to go through with it,
Their nerve appears to falter.

I see a pigeon on the roof,
They say he is just roosting,
But I can tell he is depressed,
His ego needs some boosting.

This suicidal pigeon
Is not the only one,
I've noticed lots of other birds
Who wish their life was done.

Balancing quietly on the edge
He peers beyond the brink,
He contemplates his lot in life
And feels his spirits sink.

Don't jump! I scream - which startles him
And makes him turn to flight,
Yet though this bird chose not to jump,
I know the next one might.

The Crystal Ball

The mirrored globe of glass aloft
The starlit ballroom floor,
Rotates, reflecting faces,
Of those I knew before.

A soft string palm court orchestra
Is playing at the side,
As everybody that I've known
Begins to sway and glide.

The women wearing thirties gowns,
The DJ'd men, well groomed,
The gin and tonic laughter,
The ladies hair, perfumed.

I stand amidst this mass of souls
Of people I recall,
But is it me who leads this dance,
Or they, who run the ball?

The music seems to fade away,
I float towards the ceiling,
Reflected in the mirrored globe
The images are reeling.

The throng below becomes compressed,
Then downward swings the knife,
To slice a section, wafer thin,
A portrait, of my life.

That Cow's having a Shit

I'm not in Plaistow, I'm not in Paris,
I'm not in Kathmandu,
I'm watching a cow in a Surrey field
That appears to be doing a poo.

Mickleham Memories

In Surrey hills is splendour found,
The smell of damp earth on the ground,
The dappled sunlight through the trees
That sets my troubled mind at ease.

Midst box and yew and silver birch,
The countryside becomes my church,
My soul is rising as I walk
Upon a path of flint and chalk.

The song of birds is all I hear,
Then halfway up the branches clear;
An emerald hill and valley farm,
Lie peaceful in a world of calm.

With lark ascending, so do I,
Though earthbound, still my spirits fly,
And from the top in air that's still,
View Happy Valley and Box Hill.

But Mickleham Downs remains my goal,
This place which captivates my soul,
With open softness, green and bright,
Where sunlight holds approaching night.

Yet, nearly full, there is the moon,
Whose heavenly light will be here soon;
A marble globe suspended high,
Surrounded by a crystal sky.

Across the downs through setting sun,
My time in paradise near done,
There's Ranmore, church and Thomas Tallis,
Fantasias overflow my chalice.

Silent Hounds

I stand in wealthy solitude,
The lord of all I see,
Cold mists are rolling over
Damp earth and verdigris.

My tapestries reflect the moon,
They cover dust and mould,
The stagnant moat lies still and dark,
My servant's bones lie cold.

I see my mausoleum,
White marble through the vine,
I stand in wealthy solitude
And all I see is mine.

Trouble Brewing

A pyramid shaped tea bag
Was leaving church one day
When he spied a square tea bag
Who looked a little gay

Walking down towards the park
To play a game of tennis,
But on the corner was a gang
Of round tea bags with menace.

They jostled him and called him names,
They tripped him and he fell,
The pyramid called from the church,
"Are you tea bags from hell?"

He crossed the road, confronting them,
The round bags turned and stared,
Who was this stranger who walked in
Where no one ever dared?

The pyramid spoke softly,
"It cannot be denied,
We're different shapes, but we are all
Black tea leaves deep inside".

The round tea bags helped up the square,
Their error they could see,
Then with the pyramid went home,
To make a pot of tea.

Royal Jubilee

Our Queen went to an abbey
Where a bishop placed a crown
Upon her head and since that day,
She has never let us down.

Solipsism says to us
That we are each the core,
Of a universe preoccupied
With ourselves and little more.

Our deaths can never be the end,
Religion offers life,
Beyond the grave, eternally,
Blind bigotry runs rife.

But ninety nine point nine percent
Of species small and great,
Are now extinct, so probably,
This too will be our fate.

Point one percent is all that's left
Of species, great and small;
The human mammal has evolved,
Has risen, and will fall.

Our Queen is in her gilded cage
Pursued by the lemming crowd;
Eclectic, common subjects,
Awed by a Turin Shroud.

Our DNA is ninety six
Percent the same as Chimps,
With half that of bananas,
We have the chance to glimpse

The lack of our uniqueness,
And find, a little late,
The universe has no concern,
For individual fate.

The natural world is so complete,
With so much to explore,
The multiverse so dazzling,
So why do we need more?

Our Queen has reigned for sixty years,
Today I saw her hat,
Beneath which she defends the faith,
The church has seen to that.

Retirement Home

I close the door,
Alone once more,
Have kept things in,
This was my sin,
Not given out
I had no doubt.

I didn't share,
Was always fair,
Live and let live,
But never give,
Now I'm alone
When I go home.

I planned this end
Without a friend,
Which I regret,
I sit and fret,
Alone once more,
I've closed the door.

Snow Escape

The heavy snow will deaden sound,
Reflected sunlight blind;
The screams will echo round the hills,
But no one will they find.

The snows lay thick, there are no tracks
And no one will they save;
The wind may whisper, but the hills,
Are silent as the grave.

The Doubt

I was here.
I was innocent.
I was the centre of the universe.

Ahead,
All things were possible,
All achievable.
I had all the time in the world,
I would live forever.

I knew nothing of death,
That was for others,
That was only for the very, very old.
Everything revolved around me
And moved forward with me.

But, even then, the finite fact
Would whisper.
Even then, the tiniest first shadow
Was cast upon the edge of my immortality.
The first shadow of a doubt.

Now

Pine cones and sea shells,
Sand dunes and drift wood,
Long summer days with your smile.

Now, as the shadows lengthen
Over my life, I wonder,
Where are you, now?

Nothing is Perfect

If nothing is something,
Then why do we fear
The nothing beyond us,
While we are still here?

Making something of nothing
Lacks kindness and grace,
But if time is forever
And as endless as space,

Though we quest for perfection
It will never be found,
Except in the nothing,
Without shape or sound.